Science

THE PROJECT
MAKERS

John Farndon

WINDMILL
BOOKS

Published in 2020 by Windmill Books, an imprint
of Rosen Publishing
29 East 21st Street, New York, NY 10010

Copyright © 2020 Miles Kelly Publishing

Publishing Director: Belinda Gallagher
Creative Director: Jo Cowan
Senior Editor: Amy Johnson
Designers: Simon Lee, Andrea Slane
Consultant: Ian Graham
Indexer: Marie Lorimer
Image Manager: Liberty Newton
Production: Elizabeth Collins, Jennifer Brunwin-Jones
Reprographics: Stephan Davis
Assets: Lorraine King

Cataloging-in-Publication Data

Names: Farndon, John.
Title: Project science / John Farndon.
Description: New York : Windmill Books, 2020.
| Series: The project makers | Includes index.
Identifiers: ISBN 9781538392348 (pbk.) | ISBN 9781725393066
(library bound) | ISBN 9781538392355 (6 pack)
Subjects: LCSH: Science--Experiments--Juvenile literature.
| Science projects--Juvenile literature.
Classification: LCC Q164.F37 2019 | DDC 507.8--dc23
Manufactured in the United States of America

CPSIA Compliance Information: Batch #BW20WM:
For Further Information contact Rosen Publishing,
New York, New York at 1-800-237-9932

How to use the projects

This book is packed full of amazing facts about science. There are also 11 cool projects, designed to make the subject come alive.

Before you start a project:

- Always ask an adult to help you.
- Read the instructions carefully.
- Gather all the supplies you need.
- Clear a surface to work on and cover it with newspaper.

- Wear an apron or old T-shirt to protect your clothing.

Notes for helpers:

- Children will need supervision for the projects, usually because they require the use of scissors, or preparation beforehand.

- Read the instructions together before starting and help to gather the equipment.

IMPORTANT NOTICE
The publisher and author cannot be held responsible for any injuries, damage, or loss resulting from the use or misuse of any of the information in this book.

SAFETY FIRST!
Be careful when using glue or anything sharp, such as scissors.

How to use:
If your project doesn't work the first time, try again — just have fun!

HOW IT WORKS
The tub with salt does not freeze because the salt lowers the water's freezing point.

Supplies:
The equipment should be easy to find, around the house or from a craft store. Always ask before using materials from home.

Numbered stages:
Each stage of the project is numbered and illustrated. Follow the stages in the order shown to complete the project. If glue or paint is used, make sure it is dry before moving on to the next stage.

The big freeze

The temperature at which a substance freezes can vary. In this project you can see how salt affects the freezing point of water.

SUPPLIES
two plastic food tubs • salt • spoon • warm water • marker • freezer

WHAT TO DO
1. Fill each tub halfway with warm water.

2. Stir salt into one of the tubs. Keep adding salt until no more will dissolve. Mark the tub that has salt.

3. Put both tubs into the freezer. Check them every two or three hours. What do you notice?

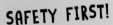

CONTENTS

Energize!

Energy is what you need to make things happen. Scientists say it is the ability to perform work. It takes many forms, but you can't either create it or destroy it. When you use energy, you simply swap it to another form.

READY OR HAPPENING?

There are two kinds of energy. Kinetic energy (KE) is energy actually doing something. It is the energy things have when they're moving. Potential energy (PE) is energy that could do something. If you're high up, for instance, you have PE, because gravity can pull you down.

The *Shockwave* jet-powered truck can scorch along at over 373 miles (600 km)/h. Moving this monster so fast involves a LOT of energy.

1 Chemical energy is stored in the chemical bonds of the jet fuel (PE).

2 As the engines burn the fuel, the chemical energy bursts out as heat energy. Heat makes gases swell and generates the thrust that drives the truck forward.

HEAT AND TEMPERATURE

Heat is the energy of molecules (tiny particles) moving. The faster they move, the hotter things are. Temperature is the way you measure how hot things are. The faster molecules move, the hotter it gets and the higher the temperature.

Extreme degrees

The lowest possible temperature is −459.67°F (273.15°C), which is called **absolute Zero**.

The highest temperature known in nature is about **50 billion°F** (10 billion°C), in large exploding stars (supernovae).

The lowest temperature recorded on Earth was **−128.2°F** (−89°C), in Antarctica.

Energy swing

You can explore the relationship between kinetic energy (KE) and potential energy (PE) with a swing. The idea is to spot when the conversions between KE and PE occur.

WHAT TO DO

1. Sit still on a swing. You currently have stored energy, or PE, in your muscles.

2. Now push off with your leg muscles and move your body to help you swing higher. You are converting the PE of your muscles into the KE of movement.

3. By moving your body, you can gain enough momentum to swing high. As you swing up, the KE turns into PE – the energy gravity gives because of your height.

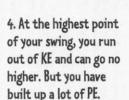

4. At the highest point of your swing, you run out of KE and can go no higher. But you have built up a lot of PE.

5. As you swing back down again and pick up speed, the PE is converted to KE. The KE will carry you right back up the other side and you will build up PE again.

As the truck accelerates, the heat energy changes to KE.

Geothermal

Heat from the Earth's interior makes steam, which is used to drive electricity generators

Hydroelectric

Falling water, typically from dams, turns electricity generators

The highest temperature recorded on Earth was **134°F** (56.7°C), in Death Valley, USA.

Force and motion

A force is a push or pull. It changes the speed, direction, or shape of something. Objects have natural inertia — they only move when forced. Once moving, they have momentum, meaning they move at the same speed and direction until forced to change.

MOTION RULES!

In the 1600s, the great scientist Sir Isaac Newton came up with three rules about force and movement, known as the Laws of Motion:

1. Things only accelerate or decelerate when forced to.

2. The acceleration depends on how strong the force is and how great the mass being accelerated is.

3. Every force or action is balanced by an equal force in the opposite direction.

FIRST LAW

Booster rockets provide the force needed to launch a space rocket. Once it reaches the right speed, the boosters can be jettisoned.

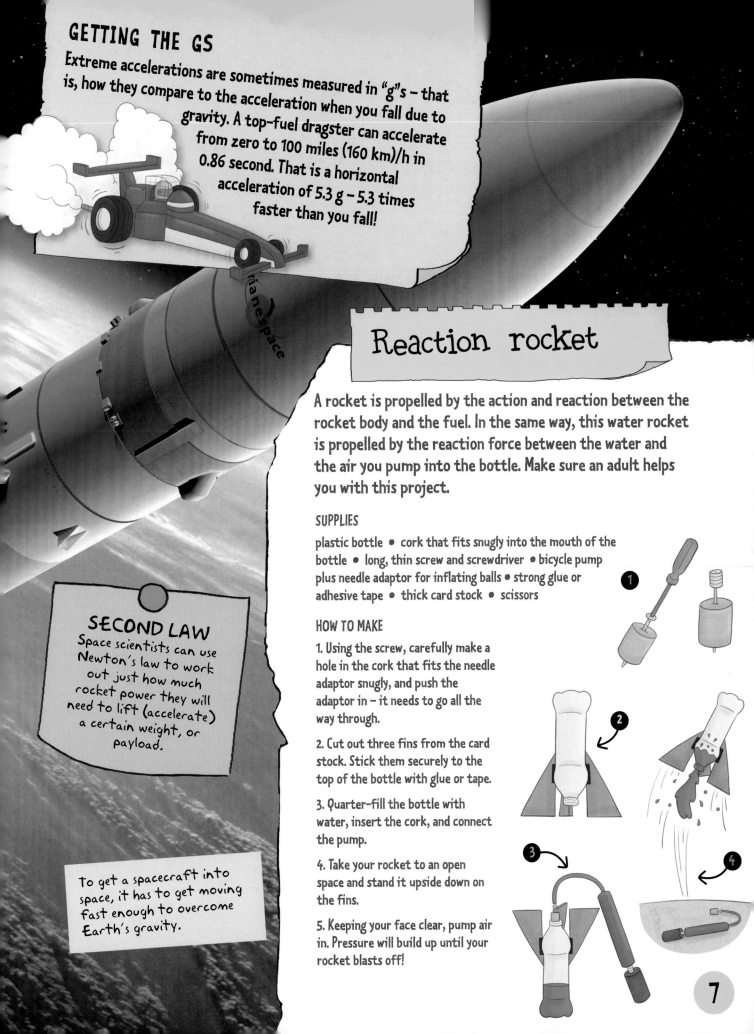

Extreme accelerations are sometimes measured in "g"s – that is, how they compare to the acceleration when you fall due to gravity. A top-fuel dragster can accelerate from zero to 100 miles (160 km)/h in 0.86 second. That is a horizontal acceleration of 5.3 g – 5.3 times faster than you fall!

SECOND LAW

Space scientists can use Newton's law to work out just how much rocket power they will need to lift (accelerate) a certain weight, or payload.

To get a spacecraft into space, it has to get moving fast enough to overcome Earth's gravity.

Reaction rocket

A rocket is propelled by the action and reaction between the rocket body and the fuel. In the same way, this water rocket is propelled by the reaction force between the water and the air you pump into the bottle. Make sure an adult helps you with this project.

SUPPLIES

plastic bottle • cork that fits snugly into the mouth of the bottle • long, thin screw and screwdriver • bicycle pump plus needle adaptor for inflating balls • strong glue or adhesive tape • thick card stock • scissors

HOW TO MAKE

1. Using the screw, carefully make a hole in the cork that fits the needle adaptor snugly, and push the adaptor in – it needs to go all the way through.

2. Cut out three fins from the card stock. Stick them securely to the top of the bottle with glue or tape.

3. Quarter-fill the bottle with water, insert the cork, and connect the pump.

4. Take your rocket to an open space and stand it upside down on the fins.

5. Keeping your face clear, pump air in. Pressure will build up until your rocket blasts off!

Pulling together

When you drop something, it doesn't just fall of its own accord. It falls because it's pulled toward Earth by a force called gravity. Gravity is what keeps us on the ground, and why the planets go around the Sun.

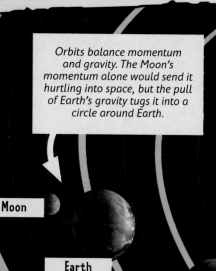

Orbits balance momentum and gravity. The Moon's momentum alone would send it hurtling into space, but the pull of Earth's gravity tugs it into a circle around Earth.

Moon

Earth

UNIVERSAL ATTRACTION

Gravity is the mutual force of attraction that holds the universe together. Every bit of matter in the universe has its own gravity pull and attracts everything else. The strength of the pull depends on how massive things are and how far apart. Objects with more mass pull more strongly than those with less.

In space, things go around each other in paths called orbits. The planets in our solar system, as well as other objects such as asteroids and comets, all orbit the Sun because it has a massive pull of gravity.

Parachute power

If there was no air, a feather would fall at the same speed as a lead weight. But air slows things down, as you can see with this simple parachute.

SUPPLIES

plastic shopping bag • ruler • pencil • scissors • thin string • two small plastic toys, roughly the same size • adhesive tape

HOW TO MAKE

1. Cut a 4-inch (10 cm) square from the bag. Using the scissors, make a tiny hole in each corner.

2. Thread a piece of string through each hole and tie it in place.

3. Tie or stick all four strings to one of the toys.

How to use:
Find a place indoors where you can drop the toys. Drop the toy with the parachute and the other toy at the same time. Which one reaches the ground first?

How it works:
The toy with the parachute takes longer to reach the ground because the parachute's large area means it hits a lot of air as it falls, slowing it down.

HEAVY!

When something is heavy, you might talk of its weight. But scientists talk only of mass. Mass is how much matter there is. For scientists, weight is a force; it's how strongly gravity pulls. Weight is measured as a force in units called newtons, whereas pounds and kilograms are measures of mass. So weightlifters should be called masslifters!

TOP OF THE WORLD

In 2012, daredevil skydiver Felix Baumgartner jumped from a capsule 24 miles (39 km) above the ground. When he first started to fall, he accelerated rapidly, reaching 849.8 miles (1,357.64 km)/h. The force of the air pushing on him (air resistance) increased as he gained speed. Eventually the air resistance became equal to his weight, and he then fell steadily at the same speed, called terminal velocity.

Earth's gravity accelerates everything down equally fast. It's said that the scientist Galileo Galilei (1564–1642) proved this with a simple experiment. He dropped two different weights off the famous Leaning Tower of Pisa – and found they reached the ground simultaneously.

Jumping from the top of the stratosphere, it took just over 9 minutes for Baumgartner to reach the ground.

Pushing it

Pressure is the amount of force acting over an area. Air and water exert pressure as they push against their surroundings. This is the combined effect of the molecules in water and air constantly moving, whizzing around at speeds of 932 miles (1,500 km)/h or more.

Pressure planet

The planet Venus has such a thick atmosphere that its pressure is **90 times** that of Earth's.

Robot vehicles may be sent to land on Venus in the future.

Venus rovers will need to be built **super strong** to avoid being quickly crushed.

UNDER PRESSURE

When you squeeze water or air molecules into a smaller space, the molecules jostle harder and the pressure rises. Similarly, adding heat increases pressure as the molecules zoom about faster and smash into things more forcefully. In a geyser, underground water is superheated and squeezed into very small spaces, creating great pressure.

Geysers are found near active volcanic areas where there is magma (molten rock) underground. The magma superheats the water, creating enough pressure to shoot out a scalding jet at the surface.

Bottle crusher

We are so used to air pressure that it's hard to imagine its power. But you can witness it for yourself in this simple experiment with steam in a bottle. It's crushing!

SUPPLIES

plastic bottle with a screw top • a little hot water • cold or iced water

WHAT TO DO

1. Ask an adult to quarter-fill the bottle with really hot water from a tap or kettle.

2. Leave to stand for a few seconds, then screw the lid on tight.

3. Hold the bottle under a running cold tap, or place in a bowl of iced water. The bottle will instantly be crushed.

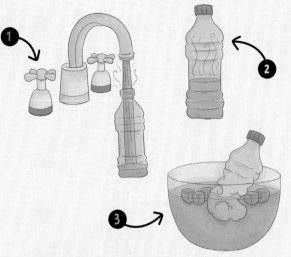

How it works:

As the cold water chills the hot air inside the bottle, the air shrinks. The pressure of the air outside instantly crushes the bottle.

KEY

1 Groundwater seeps down through tiny channels in the rock. The water comes from rain, snow, and often nearby rivers and lakes.

2 The pressure increases as the water travels further below the surface.

3 Heat from the magma chamber heats the water. Under such pressure, water reaches very high temperatures but does not boil – this is called superheating.

4 The water rises rapidly, forced through a kind of underground plumbing system of narrow channels and cracks in the rock.

5 Water and steam collect in chambers. The steam bubbles out slowly, heating the water above. The water boils suddenly, releasing pressure and spewing out water and steam.

6 In a hot spring, rising water is cooled by groundwater before reaching the surface. The pressure drops, so the water flows out steadily rather than erupting.

HIGH PRESSURE

As air rises, it cools. The molecules slow down and become tightly packed together, so the air becomes denser and starts to sink. The air presses on the Earth's surface, creating high pressure. High pressure often brings fine, dry weather.

Sinking air in high-pressure zones blows out winds and dries the air, creating clear skies.

When air gets cooler, the molecules slow down and move closer together.

Floating and flying

It's amazing that heavy airplanes can fly, and big ships can float. After all, even a tiny stone will fall through the air and sink in water. But both planes and ships use their shape to maximize the support given by molecules, which give lift in air and buoyancy in water.

ON THE SURFACE

When an object is submerged in water, it's pulled down by its weight. But the water pushes back up with a buoyancy force equal to the weight of water displaced (pushed out of the way) by the object. If the object is less dense than water, it floats. It is said to be buoyant.

3 When the weight of the displaced water equals the weight of the boat, the boat floats

1 Boat displaces a certain volume of water

2 Displaced water causes a buoyancy force

A heavy metal ship can float because its large hull pushes enough water out of the way to create a huge upthrust, enough to keep it afloat. The key is the air trapped inside the hull, which reduces the ship's overall density.

Burners add more hot air whenever the balloon needs to climb.

FLOATING ON AIR

Just as ships can float on water, so balloons can float on air. Here the balloon must be filled with a gas that is less dense than air. That way the balloon becomes naturally buoyant and rises through the air, just like a cork bobs up through water. The gas in the balloon could be helium, which is lighter than air, or hot air, which is lighter than cool air.

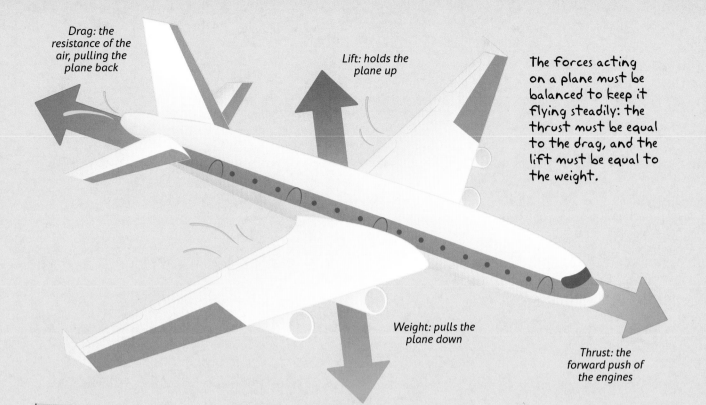

Drag: the resistance of the air, pulling the plane back

Lift: holds the plane up

The forces acting on a plane must be balanced to keep it flying steadily: the thrust must be equal to the drag, and the lift must be equal to the weight.

Weight: pulls the plane down

Thrust: the forward push of the engines

The wings of a plane have a special downcurve and slice through the air at an angle, a shape known as an aerofoil. This diverts the flow of air over and under the wings in a special way and alters how the air pushes on the wing. It pushes less on top of the wing and more from beneath, and so the wing is lifted.

The **wandering albatross** has the longest wings of any bird, up to 11.5 feet (3.5 m) across. They help give it enough **lift** to glide for hours at a time.

Sink or float!

See how shape can give a boat buoyancy by reshaping a ball of modeling clay into a boat that floats.

SUPPLIES
modeling clay • basin or large bowl of cold water

WHAT TO DO
1. Lower a large ball of modeling clay into the water.

2. You will see that the ball sinks – this is because it is denser than water. The water level rises because water is displaced by the ball as it sinks.

3. Take the ball out and reshape it to make a bowl-shaped boat with tall sides.

4. Place the clay back in the water. This time it should float, even though it has the same weight. This is because the shape displaces a larger volume of water, due to the air it contains.

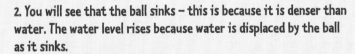

The littlest things

All matter is built up from tiny pieces called atoms. Atoms are so minuscule, two billion could fit on this period. Scientists once thought atoms were the smallest things of all, but it was then discovered that they are actually more like clouds — mostly empty space, dotted with even tinier subatomic particles.

INSIDE AN ATOM

At the core of every atom is its nucleus, a cluster of two kinds of particles: protons and neutrons. Even tinier particles, electrons, whiz around the nucleus. But don't imagine subatomic particles as tiny solid balls; they are just concentrations of energy that occur in particular places.

Nucleus

A molecule is made up of two or more atoms chemically bonded together. In this carbon dioxide molecule, a carbon atom is bonded to two oxygen atoms.

Oxygen atom

Carbon atom

Oxygen atom

The number of electrons in an atom always matches the number of protons, so an atom has a neutral electrical charge. There are eight protons and eight electrons in this oxygen atom.

FOUR FORCES

Atoms can be split, but they are usually held together by three forces – the electrical attraction between the negative electrons and positive protons and the "strong" and "weak" forces that bind the particles of the nucleus together. These three forces, together with gravity, are the basic forces of nature that hold the entire universe together.

Quark

Electrons have a negative electrical charge

The nucleus of an oxygen atom.

A proton composed of three quarks. Quarks are a very important type of particle, as they combine to make up protons and neutrons.

Proton

Scientists now have **microscopes** powerful enough to actually see **atoms**.

Neutron

Protons have a positive electrical charge; neutrons have none

The tiniest of all

By smashing atoms together at high speeds, scientists have discovered 200 different subatomic particles. They're all made from two kinds: quarks and leptons. Electrons are leptons. Protons and neutrons are built up from quarks. There are six flavors of quarks, and scientists have given them strange names.

Up quark

Down quark

Top quark

Bottom quark

Strange quark

Charm quark

It's chemistry

There's an unimaginable number of different substances in the universe. Yet they are all made up from just over 100 basic chemicals, known as elements, such as gold, iron, and carbon. Each element has its own unique kind of atom.

Elements at work

Metals are hard, dense, shiny solids that transmit heat and electricity well.

The best element at conducting electricity is **Silver**. But copper and gold are used more often in electrical equipment because copper is cheaper and gold is much more resistant to corrosion.

Noble gases

such as argon and krypton are often used to fill light bulbs because they don't react with the bulb's metal filament and burn it out the way oxygen would.

THE ELEMENTS CHART

In the 19th century, chemist Dmitri Mendeleev (1834–1907) realized that all the elements can be arranged in a chart called the Periodic Table, in order of their atomic number. Elements in the vertical columns have similar characteristics. Elements get less reactive from left to right, along the rows.

UNIQUE ATOMS

All the atoms of an element are the same. Each can be identified by its own atomic number. This is the number of protons in its atoms, from hydrogen with one to oganesson with 118. The number of protons is the only difference between elements, yet it has a huge effect on their nature.

K *Fruits such as avocados, raisins and bananas are high in potassium*

Po Ra *The radioactive elements polonium and radium were discovered by Marie and Pierre Curie, in 1898*

Ca *Chalk cliffs are made of the compound calcium carbonate*

Scientists give each element a symbol, typically its initial –
Carbon is **C**, **Hydrogen** is **H**, **Copper** is **Cu**.

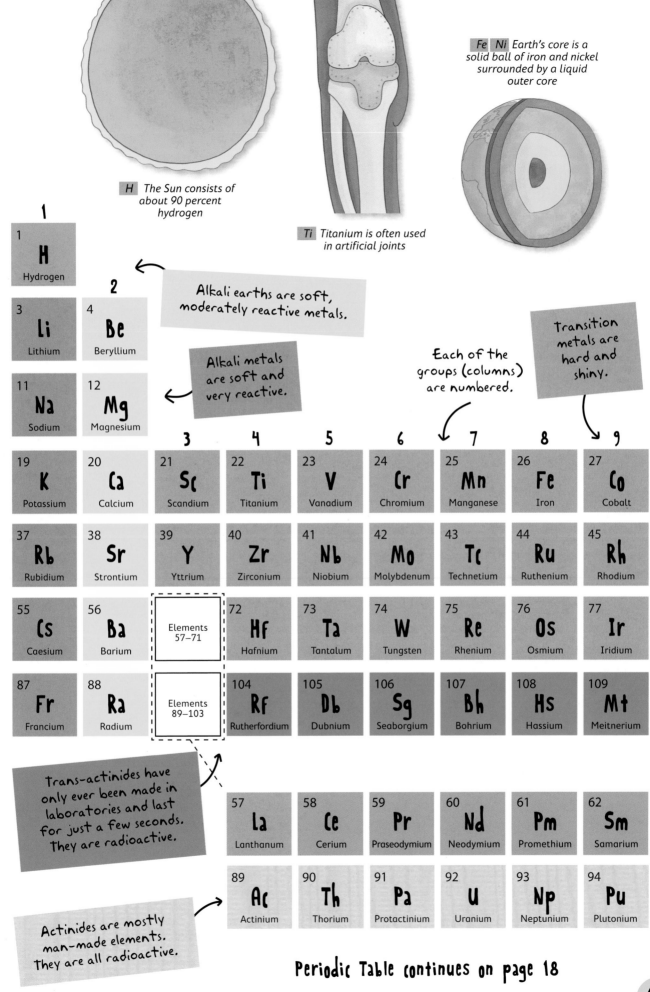

H The Sun consists of about 90 percent hydrogen

Ti Titanium is often used in artificial joints

Fe *Ni* Earth's core is a solid ball of iron and nickel surrounded by a liquid outer core

1

1
H
Hydrogen

Alkali earths are soft, moderately reactive metals.

2

3	4
Li	**Be**
Lithium	Beryllium

Alkali metals are soft and very reactive.

Each of the groups (columns) are numbered.

Transition metals are hard and shiny.

11	12
Na	**Mg**
Sodium	Magnesium

		3	**4**	**5**	**6**	**7**	**8**	**9**
19 **K** Potassium	20 **Ca** Calcium	21 **Sc** Scandium	22 **Ti** Titanium	23 **V** Vanadium	24 **Cr** Chromium	25 **Mn** Manganese	26 **Fe** Iron	27 **Co** Cobalt
37 **Rb** Rubidium	38 **Sr** Strontium	39 **Y** Yttrium	40 **Zr** Zirconium	41 **Nb** Niobium	42 **Mo** Molybdenum	43 **Tc** Technetium	44 **Ru** Ruthenium	45 **Rh** Rhodium
55 **Cs** Caesium	56 **Ba** Barium	Elements 57–71	72 **Hf** Hafnium	73 **Ta** Tantalum	74 **W** Tungsten	75 **Re** Rhenium	76 **Os** Osmium	77 **Ir** Iridium
87 **Fr** Francium	88 **Ra** Radium	Elements 89–103	104 **Rf** Rutherfordium	105 **Db** Dubnium	106 **Sg** Seaborgium	107 **Bh** Bohrium	108 **Hs** Hassium	109 **Mt** Meitnerium

Trans-actinides have only ever been made in laboratories and last for just a few seconds. They are radioactive.

57 **La** Lanthanum	58 **Ce** Cerium	59 **Pr** Praseodymium	60 **Nd** Neodymium	61 **Pm** Promethium	62 **Sm** Samarium
89 **Ac** Actinium	90 **Th** Thorium	91 **Pa** Protactinium	92 **U** Uranium	93 **Np** Neptunium	94 **Pu** Plutonium

Actinides are mostly man-made elements. They are all radioactive.

Periodic Table continues on page 18

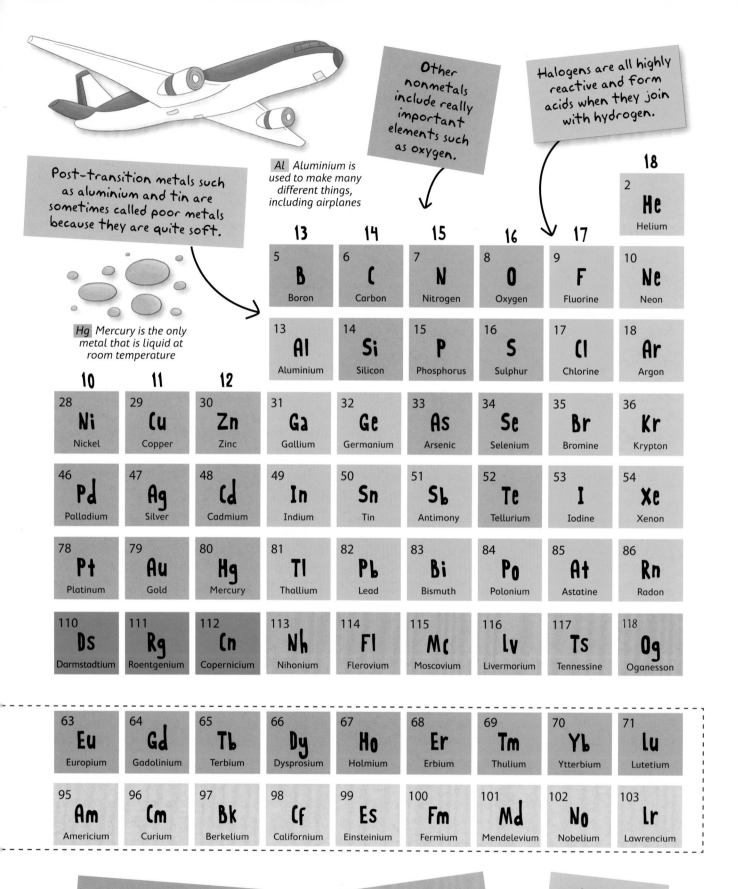

Post-transition metals such as aluminium and tin are sometimes called poor metals because they are quite soft.

Other nonmetals include really important elements such as oxygen.

Halogens are all highly reactive and form acids when they join with hydrogen.

Al Aluminium is used to make many different things, including airplanes

Hg Mercury is the only metal that is liquid at room temperature

18

| 2 **He** Helium |

13	**14**	**15**	**16**	**17**	
5 **B** Boron	6 **C** Carbon	7 **N** Nitrogen	8 **O** Oxygen	9 **F** Fluorine	10 **Ne** Neon
13 **Al** Aluminium	14 **Si** Silicon	15 **P** Phosphorus	16 **S** Sulphur	17 **Cl** Chlorine	18 **Ar** Argon

10	**11**	**12**					
28 **Ni** Nickel	29 **Cu** Copper	30 **Zn** Zinc	31 **Ga** Gallium	32 **Ge** Germanium	33 **As** Arsenic	34 **Se** Selenium	35 **Br** Bromine	36 **Kr** Krypton
46 **Pd** Palladium	47 **Ag** Silver	48 **Cd** Cadmium	49 **In** Indium	50 **Sn** Tin	51 **Sb** Antimony	52 **Te** Tellurium	53 **I** Iodine	54 **Xe** Xenon
78 **Pt** Platinum	79 **Au** Gold	80 **Hg** Mercury	81 **Tl** Thallium	82 **Pb** Lead	83 **Bi** Bismuth	84 **Po** Polonium	85 **At** Astatine	86 **Rn** Radon
110 **Ds** Darmstadtium	111 **Rg** Roentgenium	112 **Cn** Copernicium	113 **Nh** Nihonium	114 **Fl** Flerovium	115 **Mc** Moscovium	116 **Lv** Livermorium	117 **Ts** Tennessine	118 **Og** Oganesson

63 **Eu** Europium	64 **Gd** Gadolinium	65 **Tb** Terbium	66 **Dy** Dysprosium	67 **Ho** Holmium	68 **Er** Erbium	69 **Tm** Thulium	70 **Yb** Ytterbium	71 **Lu** Lutetium
95 **Am** Americium	96 **Cm** Curium	97 **Bk** Berkelium	98 **Cf** Californium	99 **Es** Einsteinium	100 **Fm** Fermium	101 **Md** Mendelevium	102 **No** Nobelium	103 **Lr** Lawrencium

Lanthanides are silvery metals, called rare earths because it was once thought they couldn't stay in the ground long without reacting.

Elements 113–118 are man-made and have only been created briefly, so their properties cannot be known for certain.

Noble gases get their name because they seem to stand aloof, not reacting.

ELEMENTS TOGETHER

Pure elements are quite rare. Most substances are compounds – made from two or more elements bonded together. The compounds are usually very different from the elements. Salt is a compound of sodium and chlorine. But sodium is a metal that fizzes and glows in water, and chlorine is a thick green gas.

O Every cell in the human body needs a continual supply of oxygen

C Plants take in carbon dioxide and use it to produce sugar for food

S The gas sulphur dioxide can be released during volcanic eruptions

The Periodic Table is constantly updated as scientists discover more elements. The most recent elements to be discovered (113, 115, 117, and 118) were officially added in 2016.

Unlike the noble gases on the right, sodium on the left of the table is highly reactive, exploding when it hits water.

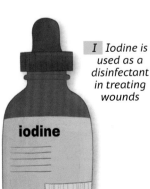
I Iodine is used as a disinfectant in treating wounds

iodine

MAKING WATER

An element is one type of atom. A compound is made when atoms of different elements join together. A molecule of each compound always has the same combination of atoms. For instance, a water molecule is always made from two atoms of hydrogen and one of oxygen.

Seawater is a mixture made up of mostly water, with a small amount of salts and other substances.

19

What's the matter?

Every substance in the universe — everything that's not just empty space — consists of matter. It has three main forms — solid, liquid, and gas. These are called the states of matter. They seem different, but they can switch from one to the other and back if the temperature and pressure is right.

A gas does not have any shape or strength, and swells to fill any space. This is because the molecules move so fast that they do not hold together.

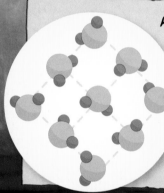

A solid has a definite shape. This is because its molecules are tightly packed and locked together in a regular structure and just vibrate on the spot. The hotter it gets, the more they vibrate.

MOLECULES AND MATTER

Every substance is made of molecules. It's the way the molecules interact that makes it solid, liquid, or gas. Water is one of the few substances that naturally occurs in all three states – solid as ice, liquid as water, and as a gas called water vapor. Liquid water can also be changed into a hot gas called steam by heating it until it boils.

A liquid flows and spreads out to take the shape of any container it is poured into. This is because the bonds between the molecules are loose enough to slide over each other like dry sand.

Uniquely, water expands when it freezes, so ice is less dense than water. This is why icebergs just about float.

SWITCHING STATES

As a substance warms up, its molecules move more and more. So it goes from solid to liquid (melting) and from liquid to gas (evaporation). As a substance cools down, the molecules move less and less. So they go from gas to liquid (condensing) and from liquid to solid (freezing).

Gallium is a metal with a melting point of 85.6°F (29.8°C). This is low enough that it would melt in the palm of your hand.

PLASMA

Plasma is a fourth state of matter. It occurs when a gas gets so hot and the molecules become so energetic that they release tiny electrical charges. This makes the gas ionized (electrically charged).

In a plasma ball, glowing loops of plasma are created by a high-voltage current surging through a noble gas.

Points of change

Water boils at **212°F** (100°C) and freezes at **32°F** (0°C).

Helium has the lowest freezing point of any substance at **-457.9°F** (-272.2°C).

Tungsten has the highest melting point of any metal at **6,191.6°F** (3,422°C).

Carbon has the highest melting point of any substance at over **7,232°F** (4,000°C).

The big freeze

The temperature at which a substance freezes can vary. In this project you can see how salt affects the freezing point of water.

SUPPLIES
two plastic food tubs • salt • spoon • warm water • marker • freezer

WHAT TO DO
1. Fill each tub halfway with warm water.

2. Stir salt into one of the tubs. Keep adding salt until no more will dissolve. Mark the tub that has salt.

3. Put both tubs into the freezer. Check them every two or three hours. What do you notice?

How it works:
The tub with salt does not freeze because the salt lowers the water's freezing point.

Getting a reaction

When you see a candle burn, metal go rusty, or a cake rise in the oven, you are seeing a chemical reaction. This is when different chemicals meet and react, changing each other to form new chemicals. Some reactions are slow and gentle, but others are explosive.

BURNING BRIGHT

Burning is a chemical reaction called combustion. When things burn, heat makes one substance, known as a fuel, combine chemically with oxygen. This makes a whole lot more heat. The fuel can be a solid, such as coal, a liquid like oil, or a gas, such as natural gas. The oxygen usually comes from the air.

Inside a firework

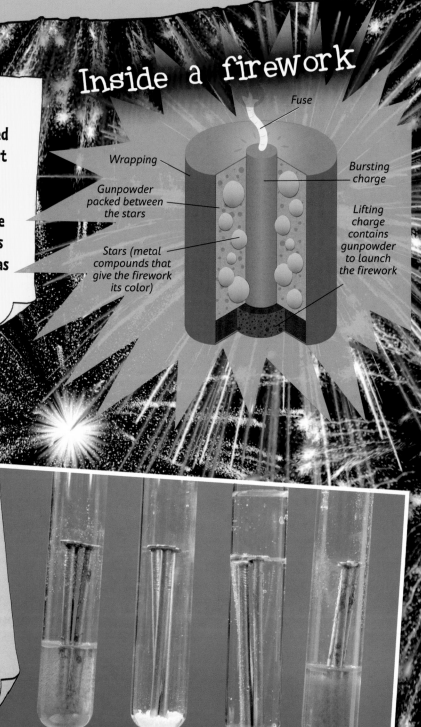

Fuse

Wrapping

Gunpowder packed between the stars

Stars (metal compounds that give the firework its color)

Bursting charge

Lifting charge contains gunpowder to launch the firework

GOING RUSTY

Rusting, like burning, is a reaction involving oxygen. This time, though, it is a slow reaction in which iron slowly disintegrates as it reacts with water and oxygen, forming a brown crust of hydrated iron oxide. Salt water speeds this up.

The nails exposed to water and oxygen (far left) and salt water and oxygen (far right) have rusted. Those in the middle have not, as they are missing water (left) or oxygen (right).

Fireworks blaze in different colors because they contain traces of chemicals such as lithium (which burns red), calcium (which burns orange), and copper (which burns blue).

Make an explosion!

You can see for yourself the power of a reaction with this simple experiment. Make sure you do this with an adult watching.

SUPPLIES

tube of Mentos • one large bottle of diet soda • goggles • sheet of paper • large open space

WHAT TO DO

1. Go out into an open space, open the bottle, and stand it on the ground.

2. Roll the paper into a simple funnel shape and place 4–6 Mentos inside.

3. Hold the funnel over the opening of the bottle and let the Mentos fall in. Now run!

How it works:

It was once thought this explosion was a chemical reaction. But scientists now think that it is caused by microscopic pits in the surface of the Mentos. The pits encourage carbon dioxide dissolved in the soda to form gas bubbles, so it is actually a physical reaction.

When nitric acid reacts with copper, it creates brown nitrogen dioxide gas and bright green copper nitrate solution.

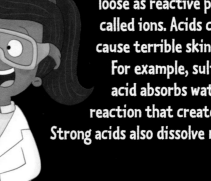

DRAMATIC ACIDS

Strong acids are extremely dangerous because they react so powerfully. Acids contain hydrogen. When mixed with water, the hydrogen atoms are turned loose as reactive particles called ions. Acids can cause terrible skin burns. For example, sulfuric acid absorbs water in a reaction that creates heat. Strong acids also dissolve metals.

23

Sparks flying

Electricity is a form of energy. It comes from electrons, the tiny particles that whiz around the nucleus of atoms. Electrons carry a negative electrical charge, which means they have an attraction to protons, which have a positive charge. Electricity is the charge on countless electrons working together.

MOVING ELECTRICITY

Current electricity is a continuous stream of electrical charge, created by a flow of electrons that have broken free from their atoms. None move far, but the current is passed on in a kind of relay. This happens only when there is a complete circuit through which the charge can flow.

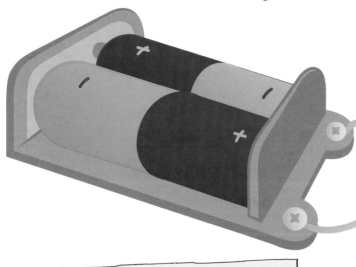

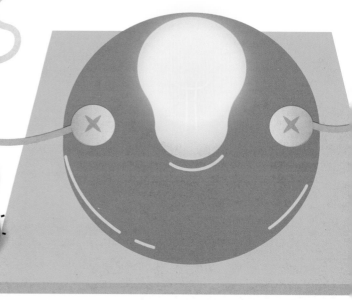

2 Wires link the parts of the circuit together, providing the pathway for the electrons to pass on the current.

1 Batteries supply direct current (DC) electricity – the current only flows in one direction. If the current constantly changes direction, it is alternating current (AC). Grid electricity is an AC supply.

HAIR RAISING

Static electricity can make your hair stand up when you comb it. It builds up when two surfaces rub together. Electrons rub off your hair onto the comb. The comb gains extra electrons, so it is negatively charged. Your hair has lost electrons, so is positively charged. Opposite charges attract, making your hair stand up.

LIGHTNING FLASH

Lightning occurs when ice crystals are flung together so violently by the air currents inside a thundercloud that they lose electrons, leaving them positively charged. The loose, negatively charged electrons gather at the base of the cloud, then are drawn toward any positive charge in a dramatic flash!

Lightning flashes brightly because the stream of charged particles heats the air to extremely high temperatures.

This simple electrical circuit has a battery to supply power, a switch to complete or break the circuit, a light bulb that glows when electricity flows, and a wire connecting them all in a loop.

3 The switch closes to complete the circuit and allow electricity to flow.

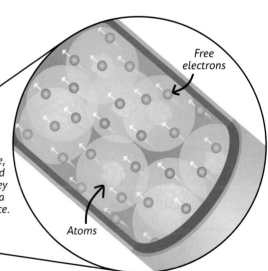

Free electrons

Atoms

4 Inside the wire, the current is carried by the free electrons. They pass on the charge like a very high-speed relay race.

Static snake

Use the power of static electricity to make this snake-charming trick! It demonstrates electrical attraction in action.

SUPPLIES

metal plate or cookie tin lid • nylon or silk scarf • plastic ruler • tissue paper • scissors • pencil • colored pens

WHAT TO DO

1. Cut out a disk of tissue paper about 8 inches (20 cm) across. Draw a spiral on it with lines about 1 inch (2 cm) apart.

2. Draw snake-like markings on the spiral with eyes at the center end. Cut it out.

3. Lay the tissue paper snake on the metal plate, then rub the ruler really vigorously with the scarf.

4. Hold the ruler over the snake's head and slowly lift. The snake should spiral up. If it doesn't work at first, you may need to rub the ruler for longer.

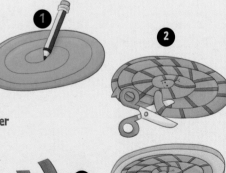

How it works:

When you rub the ruler, electrons are knocked off the scarf and onto the ruler, making it negatively charged. It's this charge that draws the snake up.

Magnetize!

Magnetism is the invisible force of attraction or repulsion between magnetic materials, such as iron. Each magnet has an area around it in which it exerts its force, called its magnetic field. The field gets weaker further from the magnet.

THE POWER OF POLES

Magnetic force is especially strong at the ends of a magnet – the poles. One is called the north pole because if the magnet is suspended freely it swings to point north. The other is the south pole. If opposite poles come together, they attract; if like poles come together, they repel.

Maglev trains have no wheels but float along the track electromagnetically.

Electromagnets in the train and guideway (track) generate a magnetic force that keeps them slightly apart. So the train is held above the track without touching it.

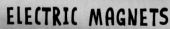

Train

Guideway

Undercarriage
of train

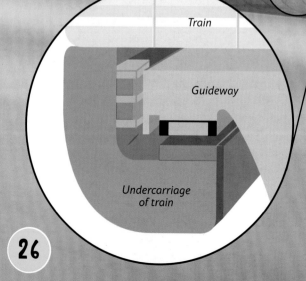

ELECTRIC MAGNETS

Electricity and magnetism are deeply linked. Every electric current creates a magnetic field around it, and moving a magnet past an electric wire generates a current in it. An electromagnet is a coil of wire with an iron core that becomes a strong magnet when the current is switched on. This is the basis for superfast trains called maglevs (magnetic levitation), which run without any wheels.

Make a compass

A compass is a device that uses a magnet to show the direction of Earth's North Pole. Here you can learn how to make your own!

SUPPLIES

bar magnet • large sewing needle • plastic bowl • cork coaster

HOW TO MAKE

1. Magnetize the needle by stroking it with the magnet 20 times in the same direction. Do this in a looping motion, lifting the magnet away between each stroke.

2. Half-fill the bowl with water, then carefully float the cork coaster as near to the center as possible.

3. Lay the magnetized needle carefully on the cork, as close to the center as you can. This makes a simple compass, and the needle should turn to point north.

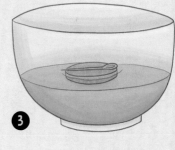

SKY LIGHTS

Sometimes the sky near Earth's poles is filled with glowing lights called aurorae. These are created by charged particles streaming from the Sun. They are pulled into Earth's magnetic field near the poles, where they collide with atoms in the atmosphere. These collisions make bursts of light energy.

Aurorae appear in the sky as dancing curtains of brilliantly colored light.

Crust

Mantle

Liquid outer core

Solid inner core

The influence of Earth's magnetic field stretches far out into space, a region called the magnetosphere.

Lighten up

We see things by light. It is radiation emitted by atoms, coming from sources such as the Sun, other stars, and electric lights. There are other kinds of radiation, but only light is visible. It always travels in straight lines so people talk about light rays, but rays are really the path light takes.

A glass wedge or prism bends normal white light so that it splits apart to reveal all the colors it contains. This rainbow is called a spectrum.

Prism

White light

WHAT IS LIGHT?

It is best to think of light as vibrating packets of energy. Light energy is emitted as tiny particles called photons. A beam of light is made of millions of photons. The color varies according to the wavelength, or the vibration pattern, of the photons.

RAINBOW COLORS

All the colors in a rainbow are different wavelengths of light. Mixed together, the colors blend into white light, which is what the light from the Sun is. But you can split them apart by refracting them (bending at an angle) through a prism to create a spectrum, or through raindrops to create a rainbow.

Each color is made by light with a different wavelength. The longest waves are red, the shortest are violet.

FAST AS LIGHT

Light is the fastest thing in the universe. In space, it travels at 983,571,056 feet (299,792,458 m)/s, and can travel from the Sun to the Earth in 8 minutes. It travels slightly slower in air, and slower still in water.

Red   Orange   Yellow   Green   Blue

Build a periscope

Light travels in straight lines – but mirrors can make it change direction. You can see this for yourself by making a simple periscope to let you see around corners!

SUPPLIES

cereal box • two small square mirrors • masking tape • glue • ruler • pencil • scissors • paints and paintbrush

HOW TO MAKE

1. Cut the cereal box so you're left with only the front or back. Copy the template (right) onto the inside. The four columns should each be the same width as the mirrors. The flaps at the ends need to be the same size as the mirrors – measure to make sure.

2. Cut out the template along the solid lines. Using the scissors and ruler, carefully score along all the dotted lines.

3. Fold along each scored line and bend into a box shape. Put glue on the tabs and stick the tabs to the sides. Secure with masking tape if needed. Stick down the flaps.

4. Put glue on the backs of the mirrors and stick one in each of the openings.

5. Paint your periscope. Once it's dry, you can use it to look over walls and around corners!

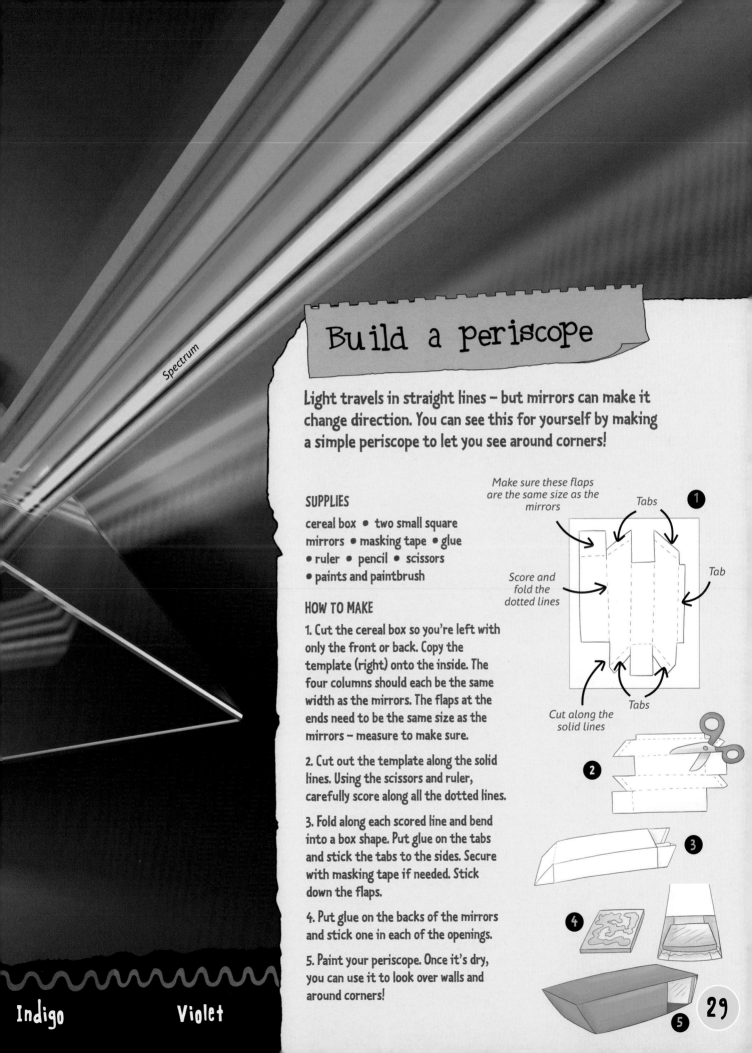

Make sure these flaps are the same size as the mirrors

Tabs

1

Tab

Score and fold the dotted lines

Tabs

Cut along the solid lines

2

3

4

5

Spectrum

Sounding out

When anything makes a sound, it sends out vibrations, or sound waves, that squeeze then stretch the air (or water). Sound waves cannot travel through a vacuum, such as space, because there is nothing to transmit them.

ECHOLOCATION

To locate things in the dark or underwater, creatures such as bats and dolphins emit high-pitched squeaks. When the sound hits something, it bounces back as an echo. From the echo, the animal can tell where the object is, as well as its size and shape.

Sound waves from the dolphin

Clicks pass through the melon

Blowhole

Phonic lips

Air sacs

Brain

Sound waves returning from the fish

Returning echoes are detected by fat-filled sinuses in the lower jaw

Inner ear

MEASURING SOUND

If sound waves are frequent, the sound they make is high-pitched. Loud sounds are made when the waves are high energy. The loudness of sound is measured in decibels (dB). An increase of 10 dB doubles the loudness of the sound you hear.

dB

| 0 | 10 | 20 | 30 | 40 | 50 | 60 | 70 | 80 | 90 | 100 | 110 | 120 | 130 | 140 |

leaves rustling

pin dropping

whisper

normal conversation

passing car

hairdryer

rock concert

fireworks

jet plane taking off

30

A supersonic jet plane flies faster than sound. Its speed is described in Mach numbers – the speed of the plane relative to the speed of sound locally. When a plane flies faster than sound, it often creates a sonic boom – a loud bang caused by the sudden squeezing of air.

The cloud of vapor shown here is a shockwave created as the plane approaches supersonic speed

THE SPEED OF SOUND

Sound takes time to travel. That's why you often see a flash of lightning before you hear the rumble of thunder it sets off. On average, it travels at 1,115.5 ft (340 m)/s in air, and slightly faster in warm air. In water, it travels much further and up to four times faster. In solids such as metals, it travels faster still.

Water music

Learn about pitch and make music at the same time!

SUPPLIES

six strong tall drinking glasses or identical glass bottles • water • thick chopstick • piano or keyboard (online will do)

WHAT TO DO

1. Fill each glass with a different amount of water. Try to make the differences fairly even.

2. Tap each glass gently with the chopstick. Do they make different-pitched sounds? Which glass makes the highest sound and which the lowest?

3. You will see that the less water there is in the glass, the higher the note (higher pitch). Try adding a little water to the glass or taking it away until they match the pitch of keys on the piano.

4. You now have your own water xylophone. Play some music!

How it works:

The glass passes on the vibrations of the stick hitting it to the water. The shorter the column of water, the higher the pitch, as the sound waves are higher frequency. So the glass with the most water produces the lowest sound.

INDEX

ACKNOWLEDGMENTS

The publishers would like to thank the following artists who have contributed to this book:

Cover Paul Boston (Meiklejohn Illustration)

Insides Sara Lynn Cramb (Astound) and Tom Heard (The Bright Agency)

All other artwork is from the Miles Kelly Artwork Bank

The publishers would like to thank the following sources for the use of their photographs:

t = top, c = center, b = bottom, l = left, r = right, m = main

Alamy 23(bl) E. R. Degginger; 26(m) Bernd Mellmann

NASA 8–9(m) NASA/JPL; 21(cr) ESA/NASA/SOHO Rex Features 9(br) Red Bull Content Pool/REX/Shutterstock Science Photo Library 6–7(m) David Ducros, ESA; 11(b) University of Dundee; 14–15(m) Mikkel Juul Jensen; 19(tr) Alexandre Dotta; 22(br) Andrew Lambert Photography Shutterstock.com 4–5(m) Santiparp Wattanaporn; 9(bl) Ana del Castillo; 12(bl) XAOC; 14(bl) Orange Deer; 19(br) EpicStockMedia; 20(m) Sergey Nivens; 21(tl) e_rik, (cr) Nikolay Petkov; 25(t) kornilov007; 27(cr) John A Davis; 28–29(m) XYZ; 31(t) Anatoliy Lukich

Every effort has been made to acknowledge the source and copyright holder of each picture. Miles Kelly Publishing apologizes for any unintentional errors or omissions.